Ledger of Tiny Losses

Ledger of Tiny Losses

poems

Katherine Lo

GRAYSON BOOKS
West Hartford, Connecticut
graysonbooks.com

Ledger of Tiny Losses
copyright © 2025 by Katherine Lo
published by Grayson Books
West Hartford, Connecticut
ISBN: 979-8-9907474-9-4

Book and Cover Design: Cindy Stewart
Cover Art: "Thin Edge of Losses" © Svitlana LeeMark, sleemark.com

For my parents

Contents

My Father Tells Me About His Dreams

Sometimes he is back in our house in Anaheim,
      sometimes with his family in Taiwan. Or, further

         back, Xiamen, port city the British gave another
name before the war. He yells in his sleep

      at the Japanese soldiers occupying his childhood,
laughs with his favorite sister's husband, who died falling

         off a ladder fourteen years ago. Time gets
mixed up, slides like language, like belief. He thinks

      in English most often but still counts in Mandarin,
language of school, when he had to ride his bike home

         twelve miles through the tropical rains of Taiwan,
their deluge unleashed at the same hour each afternoon.

      When a classmate told him about God, my father asked
if God always answered prayer. His friend said yes,

         so my father said, *I will ask him to stop the rain
today.* His friend said nothing, went home full of doubt,

      knowing God doesn't work like that. That it's not
so easy. My father pedaled home under skies that darkened

         but did not give way until he was safely inside.
When his friend later asked, *Now do you believe?* my father said,

      Yes. And it was the friend who was the most amazed.

Sister Psalm

While my sister lies on a recliner
3,000 miles away, a cocktail
of toxins dripping into her bloodstream,
Carlos is showing me a magic trick.

Other students have shown me tricks
before, bad ones, the sleight of hand
so obvious I must feign amazement.
I look at the clock, the stack of papers
on my desk, and watch as Carlos shuffles.

It's a complicated trick. He holds out
the deck and I pick a card at random.
He has me put it back and shuffle
the deck myself, which I do, that small
mean part of me making it extra thorough.

He fans the deck face up. *Do you see
your card?* he asks me. *Yes.*
He divides the deck and fans it again.
Do you see your card now? And so it goes,
until I'm not sure how he will ever find
the right one, though there must be some way
he's keeping track. Some formula to all
that dividing and shuffling.

Then he points across the room and says,
Look in the second book on that shelf.
I go and look, and there it is, my six of clubs,
buried inside a book on the other side of the room.

I tell him how good he is, and he says his mother,
who goes to church, doesn't like his tricks.
That they are something of the devil.

I think of all my prayers for my sister's healing,
how much I want God's own sleight of hand,
and how it is already here, maybe,
in Carlos's triumphant face, here

in my gasp at this holy devil reminder
of impossible things made real.

Double Delight

On the one-year anniversary of our mother's death,
after the grunting effort of digging a hole, the careful
unsheathing and loosening of the packed soil and stringy
roots from the plastic container, my sister and I stand
at the edge of our parents' driveway and stare
at the new rose bush we've just planted, neither of us
having planted anything before. *Double Delight,*
I read aloud from the tag, as if to announce it to the world.
This stalk of green with its few green leaves, the one slender
bud bending its head. When I almost run my sister over
backing out of the driveway a few minutes later,
after that shocked silence of what might have been,
we laugh until we cry, until we have to cross our legs
not to wet ourselves at the terribleness of that near-miss.
Can you imagine, my sister squeaks through hiccups,
if you had killed me on the same day Mommy died?
And I have never loved my sister more—my difficult,
exasperating, exhausting sister, whom I go for months
without speaking to. The two of us whooping like lunatics
as she clutches the frame of my rolled down window
with one hand, her other squeezing mine.

I Happen to Call My Father While He's in the Midst of a Panic Attack

his words tumbling and jamming like debris at a gutter grate. I begin the litany of questions to calm him. *Are you hurt?* No. *Are you sick?* No. *Did you eat dinner?* Yes. *You're okay, Dad. You just need some sleep.* He says *Okay.* Really, though, he's not. His brain has forgotten how to tell his body to move. The way a foot lifts, the curl of fingers. He lives surrounded by caregivers but admits he just asked them to call my brother. *For what?* I ask, but he has no answer. There is no logic to need. He's calling for someone to make it all right, leaving messages after the beep. I just bought a face cream that costs too much and went for a jog, my own panicked call to keep time at bay. All around, calls are going out. The message light is blinking. That night, I dream of a swan gliding over dark waters, looking for his chicks. They are bobbing, helpless against the current. He lifts his wing to cover them, to settle them against his white feathers, his body already turning, already floating away.

Barbershop

When her hair began to fall out,
they told my sister to go to a barber
as he would be more skilled
than the average stylist
at the delicate work of shaving
her head, at applying the razor
to her tender scalp, which has always
been covered by hair, even if
just a fine baby down,
but would now be laid bare, exposed
to light and cold and eyes
that glance away.

She sits in the chair, surrounded by men,
and explains to the barber three times
that yes, she wants him to shave it all off.
He doesn't speak much English. A father
who has brought in his son for his first cut
translates. Yes, all—*todos*. My sister points
to a photo of a muscled bald man
on the wall. *Like that.*

And so it begins, the hair falling
to the floor like soft dark grass cuttings
to be swept up and thrown away.
A pause after each row
so she can reach for a tissue
to wipe her eyes.

DNA Testing as Fortune Teller

I spit until I reach the black line
on the plastic tube, then write my name
and birthdate on the label, seal it
in the bio-hazard bag, and FedEx it back
to the lab that will tell me what diseases
are most likely to kill me. *Are you sure
you want to know?* a friend asks, and I get it,
how for some it could be an unbearable weight,
the wide lane of their future narrowing
to a sliver. But it would be nice to rule out
which diseases I *don't* have to worry about.
Besides, isn't it all guessing and chance anyway?
Like best by dates on the eggs you crack open
almost two months later, give a sniff, whisk
into breakfast. Or my friend Paul, who woke
upside down, hanging from his seatbelt
on just another ordinary drive home from work.
His car didn't make it, but no major injuries
for Paul. Just him limping a little, stunned,
the glitter of crushed glass everywhere.

We're Sorry. You Have Reached a Number

Dad, today I discovered black mold
growing under the layers of paint and old
wallpaper in the guest bathroom.
Masked and gloved, I used a screwdriver
to peel back and dislodge every loose piece
until I uncovered a whole landscape,
a map of mold continents, which
I wiped out step by step. First, a solution
of bleach and water. Next, some elbow-
grease scrubbing. Last, a mist of white
vinegar that drifted back and stung my eyes.
I will have to call the roofer. Maybe even
a contractor. This is what I would tell you
about if I could. If the number in my phone
labeled "Dad" still connected me to you.
And the thing is, even if I could, I know
you wouldn't be able to tell me what
I should do or what materials I'll need.
You would be as much in the dark as I am.
But you would sympathize with *ohs* and
wows. And when I'd tell you that on top
of the moldy wall I also got a swarm of
winged ants, you'd exclaim, *Is that right?!*
and call upon the Lord's mercy over me.
Your witness spanning the long distance
between us.

(that has been)
(disconnected)
(or is no longer)
(in service)
(if you feel)
(you have reached)
(this recording)
(in error)
(please check)
(the number)
(and try your)
(call again)
(we're sorry you)
(have reached)
(a number that)
(has been)
(disconnected)
(or is no longer)
(in service)
(if you feel)
(you have reached)
(this recording)
(in error)
(please check)
(the number and)
(try your call again)

Hello, Mom

I want to tell you about the flashing lights
on the display screen of the refrigerator
still new enough to shine, and how long

I waited on hold to schedule a repair.
All the conversations now seem to be
about what's gone wrong, what's broken,

everyone's parents especially, their bodies
a series of mysteries to test and test again,
each new specialist making a guess.

Is the medication helping or harming? Is this
a short-term crisis or the final decline?
And as they talk, I think about how,

all those years ago, I would help you dress
because it hurt you to lift your arms.
How I would mark passages of Milton

in hospital cafeterias for class and take notes
while the surgeon explained what parts
of your liver he would cut away.

What can I say to these middle-aged friends
who turn to me, asking? It is so new to them,
and I was so young the night you turned to me

and cried *I don't want to leave.* All the anger
I never felt now simmering under the lid,
the full rattle on its way.

Sorrow and I Define the Relationship

I tell her I'm not ready to commit to anything
serious, and she points out that everything

is serious with her. *True,* I say. *I guess
what I mean is nothing long-term.* Which

surprises her since I take her everywhere—
the grocery store, work, birthday parties,

dinners out with my boyfriend (though
I ask her to sit quietly in the corner).

Not to mention all those long walks
at sunset. Mornings I wake to find her

lying on my chest like a sack of wet sand,
her breath cooling my face, the sheets

sopping up her tears. *Too close?* she asks
when I roll over, retreat into sleep. I know

I haven't kept the boundaries clear,
but she's hard to resist, like a sad cat

purring in my lap. *Don't you have others
you can stay with?* I ask, and she tells me

she can go anywhere she wants, any time.
But you've made me so comfortable here.

Mark

Not everything hard will break you, but it will
probably leave a mark,

like the scratch on the front bumper
from a ladder propped against the garage wall,

the one you didn't even know you'd touched
until it started moving. Even then

a brief moment of bewilderment at this spontaneous
wobble before your brain understood

and your foot stomped the brake. That we don't
always feel the damage

is a kind of grace, the reprieve of a door pushed
against an overstuffed closet,

solid restraint to the chaos waiting to fall
on your head the minute you forget

and pull it open. *You need to face it,*
some might say, and they may be right. But first

there's laundry, and groceries, and teeth
to floss. Some Saturday, after you've said goodbye

to friends in some parking lot, you'll head to your car
and squat in the space

and light you never have in the garage,
and take a look. Long black scrape, white paint

crimped at the edges. But not bad. Nothing worth
the trouble of fixing.

Sparrows

We found them after the tree trimmers
had loaded up their machines and gone—
two baby sparrows in the grass, tumbled
like ripe fruit. We placed a shoebox on a heating
pad, lined it with soft cloth, and watched them
squeak and squirm, all purplish crepe skin,
bulging eyes shut. Our mother promised us
she'd feed them when it was time to go to school,
sugar water squeezed from a tiny dropper
into even tinier beaks. I picture her kneeling
over the box every two hours, laboring to save
what could not possibly be saved. Twenty years
later, her pale limbs swollen and still under a light
blue blanket, we too labor, squeezing water
from pink sponges into her slack mouth, more
of it dribbling out than in, love compelling us,
as it does, through the motions of giving life.

Ledger of Tiny Losses

Last night I dreamt of you
standing in the kitchen, paring
slivers of apple from its core
as you did so often, your lips
curved to grasp each slice,
the juicy crunch of it muffled
by your cheek. Only this time
you did not turn to me, your gaze
fixed on something beyond
the window, did not invite me
to share in this pleasure as you
always used to. Another entry
in the ledger of tiny losses.

Love in Middle Age

No sudden falling was involved,
nor was I swept away. The only violins
were on the radio. But every time
you laughed that bark laugh in the dark quiet

of a theater full of people not laughing, or made
me laugh, or scratched your son's back as he lay
across your lap, or talked about your daughter's
mean friends. Every time you slid your hands

into your lobster-claw mitts to pull a roast
out of the oven or flung an arm in front of me
when you braked the car too hard, thin threads
were spooling out of you. And my cautious heart,

which doesn't like loose ends, began to gather
and weave them, blue crossing red and yellow,
and where there once were only wisps is now
a solid row of squares that keeps growing and soon

will cover me. Maybe even become a necessity,
the way a blanket straight from the dryer warms
someone who doesn't even know she is cold
until the moment she suddenly isn't.

In the Movie Version

I will go through every drawer, cupboard
and dusty box of my childhood home

in a montage backed by a score that swells
just the right note of bittersweet until,

in a final dissolve, all the rooms are empty,
a clean slate I survey with welling eyes,

smiling as dust floats in the late afternoon
sun. Then I'll walk out the door,

embrace my kind and handsome fiancé,
and drive off to our new and happy

future. The one where my parents now live
in a tasteful condo at the senior community

and learn to ballroom dance. Mom will
have had clean scans for decades but still

juice organic produce, take thirty vitamins
a day, leave too many voicemails with

questions and advice about the wedding
because she refuses to text. Dad will read

and doze off in his recliner, KUSC playing
Beethoven, then go for his evening walk.

A bit slower, not quite as far, Mom reminding
him to bring his cane in case he gets shaky.

She will sit in the front row of the chapel,
tissues tucked in her sleeve. He will beam

all the way down the aisle, first time
father-of-the-bride. And the flowers, flowers

spilling their fragrance everywhere, all blush
roses in bouquets. Not a lily or wreath in sight.

Ghosts

My brother sends me a video of a man
from his neighborhood who walks just like
our father used to. Rod-straight, arms held out

two inches from his body. Maybe something
he learned, as my father did, from military
service in Taiwan. My brother caught him

while pretending to record his dog
so I could see what he sees almost every day—
our dead father on his daily walk.

Weeks after my mother died, I dropped a bag
of groceries in the middle of a Whole Foods
parking lot because I saw her backing her Ford

out of a spot in front of me. I crouched to gather
my tumbled cucumbers and tomatoes, cursing,
remembering what was no longer possible.

And it's not just the dead we see everywhere.
Today I saw one of the new teachers, dewy
with youth, praise students who looked

the same age. Herself, of course, but also me
almost thirty years ago, when an older teacher
yelled at me for using the staff bathroom

before realizing I wasn't a student. I used to be
scared of ghosts, hid under the covers from them,
sang songs to dispel them. Now I know

they're just here to remind us of what we might
otherwise grow numb to, forget. A little stab,
welling drop of ruby, proof of life.

Five Years Ago Today

My boyfriend's wife died. Brain
cancer. Of course, he was not
my boyfriend then. He was her
husband, pushing through nights
of constant waking to shoulder
her shuffling weight to the bathroom
only to find it was a false alarm.
Then the shuffle back, the settling,
until the next waking and the next.
Each time her body signaling urgent
need. One night, in the small dark
hours, he said, *Just pee the bed.*
Ghost moment that now haunts
him, like the night my mother lay
in bed, tears pooling in her ears,
the tumors growing in her bones
unbearable. I kissed her forehead,
said, *I don't know what to do,* and left.
What we're left with, when it's over,
is this knowing. The little cruelties
of failure. The hard line of limitation.
Their boat caught in a swift current,
our hand, torn raw, letting go of the rope.

Morning

Before I leave for work, I go to my stepson's
room, where the door is wide open to let in

the hallway light. He is on his side, mouth
slack, head jammed against the pillow.

I touch his arm and my mother's words
surface through the decades and tumble out—

Rise and shine! He stirs, mews a small protest,
blinks at me. *Hi,* I say. *Hi,* he answers.

How was your sleep? He swipes his nose
with the back of his hand. *Good.*

I tell him I am heading out but wanted
to wish him a good morning. He doesn't

respond, still half-submerged in dreams,
but when I stand to leave, he bolts upright,

hair jutting like quills, and holds out his arms.
Hug! he demands. I can feel his ribs, the knobs

of spine, smell his sleepy boy mustiness,
and even so new to this mother role at so late

an age, I know enough to savor this moment.
This butter and brown sugar dissolving

on a tongue that can taste such delight even
as it is hastening it to an end.

Renovation

When the workers pull up the carpet
and dissolving foam padding, we discover
Amy + Jeff 2007 TLA and a heart
my husband's late wife had painted
in white brushstrokes on the subfloor.
I read it aloud, and when I get to *TLA*,
I look at my husband, who translates,
True Love Always. Which I already knew.
When I rub his back, he says, *I'm okay.*
I'm okay. Then he scratches his head
and admits he'd forgotten about it. *Sorry,*
he adds, and I'm not sure if he's apologizing
for forgetting or for this unexpected
encounter between his two wives. I imagine
Amy in 2007, the year of her diagnosis,
kneeling on the flecked boards. She dips
the brush, maybe turns to flash a grin—
the one I've seen in so many photos—
at the tall man we both love. Her hope
for a future with him still here, their true
love always about to be covered with new
boards for our walk-in closet.

My Husband Apologizes for Having Cancer

He knows I've had enough—mother, father, sister,
not to mention all the cancer-adjacent cases, the beloveds
of our beloveds. As if he had any say. As if he hadn't

had enough himself of living with a cancer-stricken
spouse. The one before me. Of course I know he really
means he wishes I didn't have to suffer any more,

that our second year of marriage could just be figuring out
what's for dinner, whether we should buy some new chairs
for the family room. Not his body under siege, a 6-inch

incision where the surgeon had to put his whole hand in
to *feel around* and make sure the extra nub of cancer
that didn't show up in the scans was the only lurker.

So no, we're not going to Italy this summer as planned.
Yes, that. And how many future days, each spring-loaded
with their own hammer strike. But see, my darling man,

I know the risk of loving, the soft belly we must all expose
to really be alive. Even our cat, Cookie, so full of fear
she'll jump and run from the slightest thing—dropped keys,

me crossing my legs—knows that to get what she wants most,
she must uncurl and roll over, trusting there is a heart
of tenderness behind the hand reaching for her. Like her,

I'm learning how to find that one strip of sunlight slanting
through gap between shade and window ledge,
how to angle my body on its warmth.

Sorrow and I Plan a Vacation

Nowhere tropical, she cautions
between moans and little sobby sighs,

and I see her point. All that Vitamin D
would dry her right up, or even

make her strip off all those draped
layers of black sackcloth. Maybe

some Oregon coast where sea and sky
stretch in an expanse of parallel gloom

and wind-battered gulls shriek
and blow backwards. Where shells

broken by the tide lie in wait to cut
your bare foot. Better yet, a cabin

huddled at the base of ancient
redwoods grown so thick and high

their greedy leaves keep all the sun's
gold for themselves. *Oh, that sounds*

perfect! she wails, flailing a little
on the floor. I agree, don't tell her

about the meadow close by that I might
like to visit. While she's napping,

I could slip away, lie in the prickly grass,
listen to the hum of beetles and cicadas

busy in the brightness.

Chevy Impala

Burgundy car of my childhood with bench seats
wide enough to fit all four of us kids until
we grew and I had to move to the front middle,

where I held the Kleenex box and took my chances
with the flimsy lap belt and only the wide glass
before me. Cream interiors covered in plastic

that would, come summer, streak our bare legs
red when we'd peel off to get out. Steering
wheel bumped on the back for fingers to grip,

big as the wheel of a ship, ash tray stuffed
with old tissues and receipts. Car my parents
bought the year I was born and sold just after

my college graduation. Car that carried us
to school on rare rainy days, to piano lessons,
the beach. Car we sat in fighting over the radio

dial while my mother went into the store
and bought groceries. Car my father would spend
a night strapping an aluminum luggage rack

to the top with twine, then load our hard-sided
Samsonites, the wind whistling where the windows
wouldn't quite close. Car that took us on vacation

but sometimes broke down on the way, all of us
sweating on the side of a desert road while my father
lifted the hood with an old t-shirt and jumped back

from the blast of steam waiting to escape. Somehow,
between my mother feeding us sandwiches
and backyard plums from the ice chest in the trunk,

something happened and we were able to go on.
There wasn't a single drive in all those years
we didn't make it to where we were going.

My Husband Says It Hurts to Kiss Me

His lower lip cracked, his gums and the insides
of his cheeks a spiky bouquet of sores and raw
nerves. *Mucositis,* the internet tells us, from
last week's chemo. As I puree vegetables into soup,
I think about the early months of our coming together,
when we would kiss a full thirty or forty minutes
on my living room couch, away from the horrified eyes
of his children. Long, slow explorations, the warm
rasp of his tongue on mine, plump lower lip I'd bite,
tasting truffles and delight at this surprise desire,
at the world falling away so there was only us entangled,
urgent, laughing, his hands gripping my hips. Everyone
says it will get better, which I also believe, must know
to be true. But right now it's just me reminding him
to drink more water, put on sunscreen, take a nap.
Kissing him on the forehead as he winces, purses his lips
around the straw in the mug he clutches with both hands.

Like the Tree Planted

Like the tree planted by water, by a stream
pond or lake. By a river always flowing.
Roots delicate as hair growing through
the sunless earth past ants and pill bugs,
past worms and millipedes, those micro
managers of death. Past the bumble bee queen
slumbering until spring, the mole dug deep.
Until there, the cool damp, the tips extending
to drink, to send what's needed above ground
so the sticks stripped dry by empty skies
are quenched once more. First, the hard knots
bumped along the bark. Then the green blades
thrust out to catch the light. You know what's
next. The miraculous blossoms, the lush burst
of color. The heavy fruit, its juice running
down your wrist. The unseen work of patience,
of life threading its way through the dark depths.

Gravitational Time Dilation

says a body of large mass will slow
time, and clocks here on heavy earth
tick less often than clocks out in space,
clocks launched in rockets, racing far

from gravity's pull. Here, the seconds
take their time. Scientists say
the center of the earth is two and a half
years younger than its surface, and

when you feel your body flung back
during a car's acceleration, it's really
the seat pushing you forward. And
you could never see someone fall

into a black hole, should you ever find
one while hiking or on a blind date,
because time stops at the edge
of the strongest mass contained

in a certain radius, at least in the minds
of those who understand such things,
which I do not. What I do understand
is that nothing is what it seems,

and what feels like pulling might instead
be pushing, and what feels like falling
is something rising beneath you.
Your slow drift from God really

God running to meet you
to throw a robe over your shoulders,
to kiss your face and ask
what took you so long to arrive?

Acknowledgements

Alaska Quarterly Review: "Five Years Ago Today"

Bellevue: "My Husband Apologizes for Having Cancer"

Calyx: "Sister Psalm"

Gravel: "I Happen to Call My Father While He's in the Midst of a Panic Attack"

Image: "My Father Tells Me About His Dreams"

Poet Lore: "Barbershop"

Qu: "Sparrows"

Rattle: "Mark," "Gravitational Time Dilation"

River Styx: "Love in Middle Age"

South Florida Poetry Journal: "Sorrow and I Define the Relationship," and "Sorrow and I Plan a Vacation"

About the Author

Katherine Lo's poetry has appeared in *Rattle*, *Alaska Quarterly Review*, *Bellevue Literary Review*, *Calyx*, *Poet Lore*, *Tahoma Literary Review*, *Spillway*, and other journals. It has also been nominated for a Pushcart Prize. A 29-year veteran of teaching high school English, she is author of the Kirkus star-reviewed YA novel *The Cellar* and lives in Southern California.